☙ PROFILES OF GREAT ❧
BLACK AMERICANS

Shapers of America

❧❧

Edited by Richard Rennert
Introduction by Coretta Scott King

⫿⫿ A Chelsea House
⫿⫿ Multibiography

Chelsea House Publishers
New York   Philadelphia

3 5 7 9 8 6 4

Library of Congress Cataloging-in-Publication Data

Shapers of America/Edited by Richard Rennert
p. cm.—(Profiles of Great Black Americans)
Includes bibliographical references and index.
Summary: Presents brief biographies of eight individuals who
helped shape America, including Richard Allen, Mary McLeod
Bethune, Marcus Garvey, and Sojourner Truth.
ISBN   0-7910-2053-3
         0-7910-2054-1 (pbk.)
    1. Afro-Americans—Biography—Juvenile literature. [1. Afro-
Americans—Biography.] I. Rennert, Richard. II. Series.
E185.96.S427 1993   92-39962
920'.009296073—dc20   CIP
[B]   AC

❧ CONTENTS ❧

❧ INTRODUCTION ☙

by Coretta Scott King

This book is about black Americans who served society through the excellence of their achievements. It forms a part of the rich history of black men and women in America—a history of stunning accomplishments in every field of human endeavor, from literature and art to science, industry, education, diplomacy, athletics, jurisprudence, even polar exploration.

Not all of the people in this history had the same ideals, but I think you will find something that all of them had in common. Like Martin Luther King, Jr., they all decided to become "drum majors" and serve humanity. In that principle—whether it was expressed in books, inventions, or song—they found something outside themselves to use as a goal and a guide. Something that showed them a way to serve others, instead of only living for themselves.

Reading the stories of these courageous men and women not only helps us discover the principles that we will use to guide our own lives but also teaches us about our black heritage and about America itself. It is crucial for us to know the heroes and heroines of our history and to realize that the price we paid in our struggle for equality in America was dear. But we must also understand that we have gotten as far as we have partly because America's democratic system and ideals made it possible.

We are still struggling with racism and prejudice. But the great men and women in this series are a tribute to the spirit of our democratic ideals and the system in which they have flourished. And that makes their stories special and worth knowing.

RICHARD ALLEN

Religious leader and social activist Richard Allen was born into slavery on February 14, 1760, in Philadelphia. His master was Benjamin Chew, a lawyer in what was then the colony of Pennsylvania. Allen, his siblings, and his parents were household slaves who took care of the home, did kitchen work, and helped look after Chew's children.

When Allen was seven, Chew sold the entire Allen family to a farmer named Stokeley who lived in Delaware. The Allens became farmhands and spent long hours toiling in the fields. After a decade, Stokeley sold Allen's mother and three of her children, and Allen never saw them again.

Not long after the sale, Allen came upon a Methodist revival meeting in the woods near his master's home. The minister convinced Allen to see himself not as a lowly slave but as a human being who was loved by God. Allen promptly became a Methodist, and at the gatherings in the woods he often heard the institution of slavery being denounced.

One day, after his older brother and sister joined him in converting to Christianity, the teenaged Allen asked his master if Methodist preachers could visit the farm. Stokeley said yes, and several preachers began making the farm a regular stop in their travels. One of them was the Reverend Freeborn Garrettson, a former slaveholder who had become a tireless opponent of slavery. After hearing the reverend argue that slavery was a terrible sin, Stokeley decided to free his slaves.

Stokeley could not afford to release his slaves at once, so he let them buy their freedom. Allen managed to put aside some money by taking on odd jobs. Finally, when he was 20 years old, he handed Stokeley the agreed-upon sum and obtained his liberty.

Allen became an itinerant laborer in rural Pennsylvania and also began to preach. His reputation as a powerful speaker spread quickly, and several leading

Methodist evangelists soon invited him to travel with them.

In 1784, Methodism established itself as a separate denomination, the Methodist Episcopal church. Rigorous preaching, along with a spontaneous, joyous worship service, was at the heart of Methodism, and Allen believed that the combination made the Methodist church a more suitable Christian denomination for blacks than any other.

In early 1786, Allen began preaching at St. George's Methodist Episcopal Church in Philadelphia, a city where two-thirds of the blacks were free. His sermons attracted many converts; but as the number of black churchgoers rose, the white church leaders forced them to stand at the back and sides. Allen and several colleagues tried to form a separate black parish, but they were denied official permission. In response, he helped found the Free African Society, a charitable organization to address the needs of the local black community.

Meanwhile, a new seating gallery was constructed at St. George's. In November 1787, Allen and the other black parishioners went to worship for the first time in the renovated church and sat in the upstairs gallery. While they were praying, a church official told them that blacks were not allowed in the gallery. Outraged, Allen and the others stormed out of the church, vowing never to return.

For a while, the Free African Society served as a gathering place for the displaced black Methodists. But the society soon became affiliated with the Protestant Episcopal church, and many black Methodists, including Allen, did not want to abandon their denomination.

In 1793, in the midst of the struggle to establish a black Methodist church, a severe epidemic of yellow fever broke out in Philadelphia. Allen and a longtime associate, Absalom Jones, who had cofounded the Free African Society, were asked by the city's mayor to help combat the epidemic. Both men organized their black followers to minister to the sick and dying, and were commended for their efforts by the mayor and other government officials.

The following year, a black Methodist church in Philadelphia was finally established. On July 29, 1794, Allen was among the small group that gathered in a converted blacksmith shop on Lombard Street, in the heart of the city's black community, for the dedication of a new church, named Bethel.

The church's focus was to "build each other up," with Allen handling most of the pastoral responsibilities. In 1799, he became the first black to be ordained a deacon in the Methodist church. All the while, he remained eager to have Bethel be recognized as a new denomination.

In 1800, Allen married Sarah, a former slave, with whom he had six children. Now the responsibility of raising a family was added to his obligations of pastoring his flock at Bethel and earning a living as a shoemaker. But for the 40-year-old Allen, nothing was more important than lifting up his race and helping blacks gain their freedom. When a St. George's elder attempted to gain control of Bethel in 1805, Allen had his congregation pass a set of amendments, known as the African Supplement, that gave control of the church to Bethel's trustees.

Finally, in 1816, after much jockeying with St. George's for control over Bethel, the Pennsylvania Supreme Court declared that because Bethel was run by and for the black community, it should be independent. With that, Allen decided that the time had arrived for Bethel to join forces with similar black Methodist churches. On April 9, 1816, at an organizing conference at Bethel, the African Methodist Episcopal (AME) church was officially born. Allen was consecrated as the church's first bishop, thereby becoming the first black bishop in U.S. history. Moral reform, expansion of membership, and political activism to promote the civil rights of blacks became his three stated goals.

Allen promptly injected the AME church in a crisis that was affecting the black community. The American Colonization Society (ACS), an organization that sought to solve the nation's race relations problem by encouraging the return of the United States' free black population to Africa, had recently been formed. In January 1817, Allen convened a protest meeting of more than 3,000 blacks at Bethel. "Whereas our ancestors (not of choice) were the first successful cultivators of the wilds of America," the delegates declared, "we their descendants feel ourselves entitled to participate in the blessings of her soil, which their blood and sweat manured." Thus began Allen's lengthy battle with the ACS.

Among the people who fought alongside Allen were John Russwurm and Samuel Cornish, who founded

Freedom's Journal, the first newspaper in America to be owned and published by blacks. Allen contributed a number of articles to the paper, calling for the abolition of slavery and attacking the ACS's colonization efforts. *Freedom's Journal*, in turn, helped publicize the activities of the AME church among the nation's black population.

In 1819, Congress granted a large sum of money to the ACS to build a settlement on Africa's west coast. Three years later, the first black American settlers crossed the Atlantic and established the West African colony of Liberia. Allen remained an outspoken opponent of the ACS, however, and by 1830 fewer than 2,000 people were lured into sailing for Africa.

And so Allen molded the AME church into a political force. He added to its clout by establishing branches in Massachusetts, New York, Ohio, western Pennsylvania, and South Carolina. America's black communities needed a mouthpiece for making their views known to the world, and the AME church provided it.

In 1830, Allen invited black community leaders across the country to come to Bethel for the first national convention of black Americans. The gathering took place on the night of September 15, with 40 persons from seven states in attendance. Travel restrictions on free blacks kept the number of attendees on the low side. Nevertheless, they organized a national network of black support and cooperation, calling their association the American Society of Free Persons of Colour.

Allen, who was elected the society's president, worked tirelessly on behalf of the new association,

urging blacks to become more politically and eco-
nomically organized and to step up the fight against
slavery. Later in 1830, he formed the Free Produce
Society and its affiliate, the Free Cotton Society, in
an effort to strike a blow against the South's slave
economy. Members of these two groups pledged to
buy only goods made and raised by nonslaveholders.

Allen's efforts to serve his people were cut short by
illness, and on March 26, 1831, he died at his Philadelphia home at the age of 71. Today, Bethel Church still
stands in Philadelphia, the mother church of African
Methodism and a memorial to Richard Allen's dedication to the cause of black Americans.

MARY MCLEOD BETHUNE

An inspirational educator and adviser to America's leaders, Mary McLeod Bethune was born Mary Jane McLeod in Mayesville, South Carolina, on July 10, 1875. She was the 15th of 17 children born to Samuel and Patsy McIntosh McLeod, who were former slaves. Most of the McLeod children had been sold into slavery on nearby plantations, but the entire family was reunited shortly after the Civil War ended in 1865.

Handed their freedom, the McLeods built their own cabin on a piece of land near Mayesville, and Mary was born and raised there. From an early age, she was expected to work all day in the cotton fields with the rest of the family, then do chores back at the cabin. At the time, there were few schools for blacks in the South; many southerners opposed educating blacks because they wanted them to remain subservient to whites.

But in 1882, Emma Wilson, a black educator, founded a mission school for black children in Mayesville, five miles away from Mary's home. The youngster walked to the school each day to study reading, writing, arithmetic, and the Bible. She graduated in 1886, and a year later Wilson offered her a scholarship to Scotia Seminary (now Barber-Scotia College), a school for black women in Concord, North Carolina.

The blacks and whites who made up Scotia's faculty provided Mary with her first example of interracial cooperation. She trained to become a teacher and, she hoped, a missionary in Africa. When she graduated from Scotia in 1894, she applied for admission to the Moody Bible Institute in Chicago, which trained missionaries. Moody awarded her a scholarship, and that summer 19-year-old Mary McLeod moved to Chicago to begin her Bible studies as the school's only black student. In her free time, she visited prisoners at police stations, went to the slums and offered counseling to the needy, and traveled in the Midwest with Moody students to establish Sunday schools.

After graduating from Moody, McLeod learned that there were no openings in Africa for black missionaries. So she returned to Mayesville, became

Emma Wilson's teaching assistant, and was hired a year later to teach at the Haines Normal and Industrial Institute, a school for black children in Augusta, Georgia.

There McLeod organized an unusual Sunday school program for her pupils. They visited children in nearby shacks and gave them baths and distributed clothing, soap, toothbrushes, and other personal hygiene items. "Africans in America needed Christ and school just as much as Negroes in Africa," McLeod realized. "My life work lay not in Africa but in my own country."

After a year at Haines, McLeod moved to the Kindell Institute in Sumter, South Carolina, where she met her future husband, Albertus Bethune, who was also a teacher. They were married in May 1898 and moved to Savannah, Georgia. Their only child, Albertus McLeod Bethune, was born on February 3, 1899.

Half a year later, Mary McLeod Bethune was asked to join the staff of a Presbyterian church school in Palatka, Florida. Her husband encouraged her to go to Palatka, where she organized a Sunday school program, sang to prisoners in the jails, and began what would be a part-time occupation for the rest of her life: selling insurance policies for the Afro-American Life Insurance Company.

As the Palatka school expanded, Bethune began to think about forming her own school. In 1904, she learned that the Florida East Coast Railway was being built. Black laborers were gathering from all over the South in Daytona Beach, 50 miles from Palatka, to begin work on the railroad, and their children would need an education.

Sensing that she might be able to muster support for a school from wealthy winter residents, Bethune moved to Daytona Beach. She succeeded in getting the backing to open a school, and on the morning of October 4, 1904, the Daytona Normal and Industrial Institute for Negro Girls held its first classes. The schoolhouse was a two-story cottage near the railroad tracks that she rented with a down payment of $1.50, which was all the money she had.

Students were charged 50 cents a week for tuition. They were taught basic skills and crafts and were instructed in the three R's. Bethune also spoke to them about the contributions that blacks had made to African and American cultures. At the heart of her curriculum was black pride, self-respect, and faith in God.

Before long, Bethune was reaching out to the area's entire black community. The school, which had already started to accept boarders, began to offer evening courses for adults and counseling for married couples. Within several years, the Daytona Institute had 250 pupils and needed more space and supplies.

Bethune found it hard to make ends meet. "I saw that our only solution was to stop renting space," she said, "and build our own college." She promptly sought donations from her adult students' wealthy employers.

On land that had formerly been a city dump and that Bethune had purchased with a down payment of $5, she oversaw the construction of a brick building to house her school. In October 1907, the school finally moved to its new home, Faith Hall, even though the building was not yet finished.

Meanwhile, Bethune continued to improve the school. She taught her students how to grow crops and established extensive gardens. Each Sunday, she took some of her students to a nearby migrant labor camp to teach the children and counsel their parents at what became known as the Tomoka Mission. Within five years, she had established a chain of similar missions in the area.

In 1908, the growing male enrollment at Bethune's school prompted her to change its name to the Daytona Educational Industrial Training School. Shortly afterward, her husband left her and returned to South Carolina. He died from tuberculosis in 1919 without ever seeing his wife again.

On her own, Bethune began to tour the North and publicize her school to church groups and charitable organizations. Over the years, these trips attracted the patronage of a number of benefactors, including John D. Rockefeller, Sr., who paid the tuition of Bethune's most promising students, and industrialist Andrew Carnegie, who helped her build a small hospital on the school grounds.

Bethune was in the process of expanding the institute beyond eight grades and having it accredited as a high school when World War I broke out. U.S. vice-president Thomas Marshall invited her to Washington, D.C., to discuss racial segregation as it related to the war effort. Largely through her efforts, the American Red Cross decided to integrate its services and allow blacks to perform the same services as whites.

During these years, the Daytona Institute continued to expand; but Bethune knew she needed to put the school on a firmer financial footing. Finally, in 1923, she agreed to a merger with the Cookman Institute, a school for black males in Jacksonville, Florida. The new school was renamed the Bethune-Cookman Institute.

Bethune was active in several black women's clubs, most notably the National Association of Colored Women (NACW), the country's leading organization for black women; she became president in 1924 and held the post for five years. She also served as vice-president of the National Council of Women, a confederation of women's organizations. Through these groups, she became a nationally known figure. In 1928, she was invited by President Calvin Coolidge to participate in a White House conference on child welfare, and in 1929 President Herbert Hoover named her to the National Commission for Child Welfare.

As the United States became mired in the Great Depression of the 1930s, Bethune decided to form a group that would join together all the black women's clubs and organizations to address national issues affecting black citizens. In December 1935, she founded the National Council of Negro Women.

That year also saw Bethune attain a number of personal honors. She received the Spingarn Medal from the National Association for the Advancement of Colored People (NAACP). And when President Franklin D. Roosevelt named her in 1935 to head the

Division of Negro Affairs within the National Youth Administration (NYA), created to combat unemployment among young Americans, she became the first black woman to head a federal agency. Five years later, she became vice-president of the NAACP.

In the last portion of her life, Bethune helped to establish a pilot training program at the Tuskegee Institute, served as a delegate to the conference that established the United Nations, and was appointed by President Harry S. Truman to a federal committee that helped bring about full racial integration in the armed forces.

Mary McLeod Bethune died in Daytona Beach on May 18, 1955, shortly before her 80th birthday. She was buried on the campus of Bethune-Cookman College, an ongoing monument to her work for black advancement.

FREDERICK DOUGLASS

Abolitionist leader Frederick Douglass was born into slavery as Frederick Bailey in February 1818 on a farm near Easton, on Maryland's Eastern Shore. His mother was a slave named Harriet Bailey. He knew little about his father beyond the fact that he was white, although it was rumored that his mother's master, Captain Aaron Anthony, had sired him.

Bailey began working in the fields at age six. Conditions for slaves were miserable under Captain Anthony, who denied them adequate food, clothing, and shelter, and often beat them. In 1826, Bailey was sent to Baltimore to be a house slave for relatives of the Anthonys. His new masters were Sophia and Hugh Auld, who owned a shipyard. Bailey ran errands for the family and helped look after the Auld's infant son.

Sophia Auld grew fond of the young slave and often read to him from the Bible. She even began to teach him how to read, but her husband ordered her to stop because he believed that slaves should not be taught to read and write. Upon hearing his master's outburst, Bailey concluded that learning to read and write was the pathway to freedom. He immediately set about reading parts of books and newspapers whenever he could and exchanging pieces of bread for lessons from the poor white children he met on his errands. He learned to write at his master's shipyard; he watched workmen label timbers and masts, then furtively copied the letters.

When Bailey was 12, he managed to buy a copy of *The Columbian Orator*, a collection of essays that discussed the evils of slavery. He learned for the first time of the existence of abolitionists—men and women fighting to end slavery—and he began to dream of his own emancipation. "I had penetrated to the secret of all slavery and oppression," he said later. "Slaveholders are only a band of successful robbers."

Three years later, Bailey was sent to work as a field hand on a farm owned by Hugh Auld's brother, Thomas, near the old Anthony plantation. Thomas

Auld was a cruel master who beat and starved his slaves, and Bailey was often whipped for being difficult to control. To break Bailey's spirit of resistance, Auld sent the teenager to Edward Covey, a poor farmer who was often asked by richer farmers to train their slaves to be obedient workers.

Bailey did backbreaking labor for Covey for a year and was often whipped. He was then sent to another farm to work as a field hand. His new master, William Freeland, was relatively kind, but Bailey was now completely determined to gain his freedom. He started a school and began to plot his escape to the North, where slavery was illegal.

In 1836, just before Easter, as Bailey and five other slaves prepared to flee, they were seized and thrown in jail. One of their associates had exposed the plot. When slave traders came to the jail to look him over, Bailey feared he would be sold to a plantation in the Deep South, where life for a slave was said to be unbearably harsh. To his surprise, Thomas Auld appeared at the jail, had him released, and returned him to Hugh and Sophia Auld in Baltimore.

By now, 18-year-old Bailey was 6 feet tall and immensely strong. Auld sent him to the shipyard to learn the trade of caulking the seams of a boat. He was soon skilled enough at sealing these seams to seek employment on his own. Auld, however, kept most of Bailey's earnings.

In his spare time, Bailey met with a group of educated blacks who had formed an association called the East Baltimore Mental Improvement Society. He began to hone his debating skills at the society's meetings, and at one of them he met Anna Murray, a free black who was a servant for a wealthy Baltimore family. They became engaged in 1838.

Meanwhile, Bailey, still longing for freedom, began to plan another escape to the North. On September 3, 1838, disguised as a sailor, carrying money borrowed from Anna, and armed with a friend's document that identified him as a free seaman, he boarded a train going north. He arrived in New York City the next day and found shelter with David Ruggles, who was part of the Underground Railroad, the network of people who harbored runaway slaves and helped them escape to safe areas in the northern United States and Canada.

The 20-year-old runaway slave immediately sent for Murray, and they were married on September 15; they eventually had four children. Ruggles helped them escape farther north, to the port of New Bedford, Massachusetts, where they stayed with Nathan Johnson, a well-to-do black man. Bailey, deciding that a new name might help him avoid being captured, changed his surname to Douglass, after a character in a Sir Walter Scott novel that Johnson was reading.

In New England, Douglass was quickly drawn into the abolitionist movement. He joined the American Anti-Slavery Society, led by William Lloyd Garrison, who edited the popular antislavery newspaper *The Liberator*. "The paper became my meat and drink," Douglass recalled.

In 1841, he met Garrison for the first time, at an abolitionist meeting in New Bedford. A few days later, Douglass addressed the Anti-Slavery Society. Impressed by the former slave's speech, Garrison invited him to travel throughout the North and lecture audiences on the society's behalf.

Douglass's skills as an orator brought him acclaim. Some people doubted, however, that he was telling the truth about his upbringing because he sounded so well educated. To silence these critics, he decided to write his life's story. *Narrative of the Life of Frederick Douglass*, featuring introductions by Garrison and Wendell Phillips, another abolitionist leader, was published in May 1845. The book quickly became a best-seller in the North; European editions also sold well.

Suddenly famous but still a fugitive slave, Douglass decided to seek refuge in England and at the same time win Europe's support for the antislavery movement. He headed overseas in the summer of 1845 and remained abroad for two years, drawing enthusiastic crowds everywhere he spoke. He returned home only after two English friends purchased his freedom for $710.96.

In late 1847, Douglass moved his family to Rochester, New York, and began to issue the *North Star*, a weekly abolitionist newspaper that also supported equal rights for women. It attracted a wide readership and helped him grow in stature. He continued to publish the paper for 16 years.

The abolitionist cause, however, was not making many gains. In 1850, the U.S. Congress passed the Fugitive Slave Act, which strengthened earlier laws requiring that runaway slaves be returned to their owners. Seven years later, the U.S. Supreme Court declared in the Dred Scott decision that slaves "had no rights which the white man was bound to respect."

In response, Douglass became part of the Underground Railroad, and his home in Rochester became an important stop on the line. And when the Civil War erupted in April 1861, he announced that he would fight for the emancipation of all slaves in the Confederacy and the Union border states, and the right of blacks to enlist in the armies of the North. President Abraham Lincoln even held two private meetings with Douglass.

Clearly the nation's leading black spokesman, Douglass vowed after the Civil War ended in 1865 to help his race secure the right to vote. He traveled throughout the North, and the black suffrage movement grew. In 1868, the Fourteenth Amendment, guaranteeing blacks their full rights as citizens, was ratified. Two years later, the Fifteenth Amendment guaranteed all male citizens the right to vote, regardless of race.

Also in 1870, Douglass took over the *New National Era*, a newspaper based in Washington, D.C., and in 1874 he accepted an offer to become president of a bank for black investors. After the Freedmen's Saving and Trust Company failed, he returned to the lecture circuit, giving speeches on a variety of topics, including Scandinavian folklore. Many people described him as one of the world's greatest speakers.

In 1877, Douglass was awarded a political post, U.S. marshal for the District of Columbia. Three years later, he was appointed recorder of deeds for the capital city. Both jobs afforded him ample time for writing and speaking engagements, and in 1881 he published another autobiography, *The Life and Times of Frederick Douglass*. Never one to avoid controversy, he married Helen Pitts, a white woman who was 20 years his junior, in 1884, two years after Anna Douglass died.

Douglass's final political appointment came in 1889, when he was named ambassador to Haiti, a position he held for two years. He spent his last years seeking to awaken the nation's conscience to the growing number of violent crimes that were being committed against blacks.

Frederick Douglass was in Washington, D.C., on February 20, 1895, when he died of a heart attack at the age of 77. With his passing, one of America's most eloquent voices for human rights was silenced.

W. E. B. DU BOIS

$\mathbf{S}$cholar and activist William
Edward Burghardt Du Bois was born on February 23,
1868, in Great Barrington, Massachusetts. Shortly
after William's birth, his father, Alfred Du Bois, abandoned his family. William and his mother, Mary,
never heard from the elder Du Bois again.

An excellent, highly motivated student, young Du
Bois held odd jobs after school to supplement his

mother's income as a domestic servant. He graduated from Great Barrington High School in 1884 with the intention of going to Harvard College, but he lacked the funds. The following year, four towns-people raised enough money for him to attend Fisk University, a black college in Nashville, Tennessee.

Du Bois settled in quickly at Fisk, excelling academically and editing the school newspaper, the *Fisk Herald*. During summer vacations, he taught in a small rural school for blacks in eastern Tennessee. There he experienced the grinding poverty that plagued southern blacks. His work with the rural poor inflamed his social conscience, and "a life that shall be an honor to the Race" became his publicly stated goal.

Du Bois graduated as valedictorian from Fisk in 1888, then enrolled at Harvard. He graduated with honors in philosophy from Harvard in 1890, and two years later he received a master of arts degree from the school. He then was awarded a grant to study for two years at Friedrich Wilhelm University in Berlin.

When Du Bois returned from Germany in 1894, he taught for a year at Wilberforce University, a black institution in Ohio, while he completed his doctoral dissertation on the slave trade. He received a doctorate in philosophy from Harvard the following year. And in 1896, his dissertation became his first published book.

That same year, Du Bois wedded Nina Gomer, a student at Wilberforce. They remained married for 54 years, until Nina's death in 1950. The next year, Du Bois wedded Shirley Graham, one of his former graduate students. He had two children: a son, Burghardt, who died in 1899 at the age of two; and a daughter, Yolande, who was born 16 months later.

In the summer of 1897, Du Bois left Wilberforce to teach at the University of Pennsylvania and to research the social structure of a black neighborhood in Philadelphia. His landmark sociological study, *The Philadelphia Negro* (1899), called on the "black aristocracy" to help its brethren. Blacks would emerge from oppression, he concluded, only after strong black leaders stepped forward.

Du Bois's scholarship continued in the fall of 1897, when he joined the Atlanta University faculty and organized a series of annual conferences that examined the problems facing black Americans. In 1900, he put together an exhibit on black American life at the Paris Exposition. It won the grand prize and added to his growing international reputation as a scholar and a champion of black America. The turn of the century also saw Du Bois devote himself to the cause of a free Africa leading to worldwide unity among blacks; he would eventually become known as the father of this cause, Pan-Africanism.

In 1903, Du Bois published the now-classic *The Souls of Black Folk*, a powerful collection of 14 essays that probed the black American's plight. "One ever feels his twoness—an American, a Negro," Du Bois wrote. "Two souls, two thoughts, two unreconciled strivings, two warring ideals in one dark body, whose dogged strength alone keeps it from being torn asunder."

But of all the points Du Bois made in the book, the one that attracted the most attention was his criticism of educator and racial spokesman Booker T. Washington's accommodationist policies. Washington maintained that blacks should not seek social change until they had raised their economic status—a sticking point that gained him the trust of white leaders. Du Bois countered that blacks should be granted their full civil rights. He called on the educated black elite—the Talented Tenth—to provide strong leadership in the fight for racial justice, declaring, "The problem of the twentieth century is the problem of the color line."

Over the next few years, Du Bois continued to write articles for leading periodicals and published several scholarly books. Meanwhile, he attempted to unify Washington's opponents behind the Niagara Movement, a black protest organization created to promote "aggressive action on the part of men who believe in Negro freedom and growth." Washington successfully withstood Du Bois's challenge for leadership of black America; but this victory did not stand for long.

In 1910, Du Bois left Atlanta University and cofounded the National Association for the Advancement of Colored People (NAACP) in New York City. He became the organization's director of publicity and research, and served as editor of its monthly publication, the *Crisis*, a militant journal that transformed the NAACP into the nation's most powerful civil rights organization. Within a decade, the *Crisis* was boasting a circulation of more than 100,000.

Du Bois was, without any doubt, the driving force behind the *Crisis*. He used its pages to speak bluntly about racial issues and continue his criticism of

Booker T. Washington's accommodationist policies. By the time Washington died, Du Bois was being hailed as the country's foremost black leader.

In the early 1920s, Du Bois turned his attention to a new opponent: Marcus Garvey, the black nationalist leader who won thousands of supporters through spectacular parades and conferences dominated by showmanship and rhetoric. The aim of Garvey and the organization he founded, the Universal Negro Improvement Association (UNIA), was to increase black pride and promote racial separatism instead of the integration that Du Bois and the NAACP favored. The *Crisis* editor, in fact, labeled Garvey "the most dangerous enemy of the Negro race"; and by the mid-1920s, Du Bois's attacks had helped expose the UNIA leader as something of a fraud.

The *Crisis*, with which Du Bois's name will be forever linked, played a leading role in the 1920s in promoting the black cultural movement that became known as the Harlem Renaissance. By the 1930s, however, Du Bois was filling the *Crisis* with a number of his more radical views. When in the January 1934 issue he called for blacks to take advantage of racial segregation by supporting solely black enterprises, his use of the phrase "voluntary segregation" offended many NAACP leaders. Du Bois promptly resigned from his post and returned to Atlanta University to become chairman of the sociology department and resume his wide-ranging scholarly work.

Du Bois reeled off several influential books: *Black Reconstruction* (1935); *Black Folk Then and Now* (1939); and his autobiography *Dusk of Dawn* (1940). Whenever he was not at his writing desk or in the classroom, he was busy championing racial harmony around the globe, especially in Africa. In 1945, for example, he served as a consultant to the U.S. delegation attending the founding conference of the United Nations.

Du Bois's later years were marked by a flurry of activity. He returned to the NAACP for three years as director of special research. He continued his support of Pan-Africanism and attended a number of peace conferences at home and abroad.

In 1950, the 82-year-old Du Bois campaigned unsuccessfully for the U.S. Senate. That same year, his association with alleged Communists resulted in his being indicted by the federal government for failing to register as an agent of the Soviet Union. He was acquitted of all charges in the ensuing trial; yet the government refused to let him travel abroad during much of the 1950s because of his supposed ties with Communist nations. Acquitted of all wrongdoing, Du Bois's name remained tarnished, and his influence on black affairs diminished steadily.

Forced to remain on the sidelines while the civil rights struggle pushed ahead in the late 1950s, Du Bois occupied himself by writing three novels. In 1959, he was finally allowed to leave the country. He went to the Soviet Union, where he held talks with Soviet premier Nikita Khrushchev, received an honorary doctorate from Moscow University, and was awarded the Lenin Peace Prize. He then traveled to China and met with Communist party chairman Mao Tse-tung.

In 1961, shortly after joining the American Communist party, Du Bois moved to the African nation of Ghana. Another skirmish with the U.S. government caused him to renouce his American citizenship and become a Ghanaian citizen. He died in Accra, Ghana, on August 27, 1963, after devoting nearly a century to ending America's racial crisis.

MARCUS GARVEY

Marcus Garvey was born on August 17, 1887, in St. Ann's Bay on the British colony of Jamaica. He was the 11th child of Sarah and Marcus Garvey, a man of tremendous intellect who worked as a stonemason.

Young Marcus received his education in public schools and from private tutors. He especially enjoyed borrowing books from his father's extensive library.

At the age of 15, he left school to work as an apprentice in his godfather's printing shop. Three years later, he moved to Jamaica's capital of Kingston to work as a printer. There he became fully aware of racial divisions in Jamaican society and developed a strong interest in helping the country's poor blacks, who made up 80 percent of the population.

In 1909, Garvey entered Kingston's intellectual circles as a member of the National Club, a group organized to fight the problems created by British rule. He helped publish the club's newspaper, *Our Own*. He then launched his own periodical, *Garvey's Watchman*. He soon realized that if he wanted to improve the lives of his fellow blacks, the effort would take more money than he could raise on Jamaica. Believing that he could earn more money abroad, he sailed to Costa Rica in 1910.

Garvey landed a job on a banana plantation, confident that he could save enough money to return to Jamaica and lead the struggle for black rights. Instead, the poor working conditions on the plantation inspired him to start a newspaper that agitated for the rights of the plantation's many migrant laborers. It met with little success, however, and so he decided to go elsewhere. He traveled to a number of South and Central American nations, where the same scene repeated itself: he found migrant workers performing backbreaking labor. He campaigned to improve the lot of the workers wherever he went but was constantly opposed by government authorities, who viewed him as dangerous.

In 1912, Garvey decided to take his battle to the seat of the British Empire and set sail for England. In

London, he supported himself as a dockworker and attended evening classes at Birkbeck College, a school for working-class people. His studies led him to accounts of Europe's centuries-long domination of Africa and prompted him to seek out other blacks who shared his growing conviction that blacks throughout the world were one people and that Africa was their homeland.

Garvey's thinking was further stirred after he came across a copy of *Up from Slavery*, educator and racial spokesman Booker T. Washington's autobiography. Washington's rags-to-riches story—which included his founding of the black industrial school Tuskegee Institute and his program for racial progress through accommodation—had an electrifying effect on Garvey. After reading the book, he said later, "My doom— if I may so call it—of being a race leader dawned on me."

Garvey returned to Kingston in 1914 and founded the Universal Negro Improvement Association (UNIA). Its purpose was to unite Jamaica's black population with a spirit of racial pride and a program of educational and economic opportunity. The UNIA also vowed to work for the end of colonial rule and the establishment of independent black-led nations in Africa. Garvey, who became the UNIA's president and chief recruiter, intended it to be the standard-bearer of international black protest.

In March 1916, Garvey arrived in New York City and attempted to gain support for the UNIA abroad. He settled in Harlem, the district that had recently become the center of the city's black population, and found work as a printer. In his free time, he spoke on street corners, explaining his program for racial solidarity to anyone who would listen.

Within three months, Garvey saved enough money to embark on a lecture and fundraising tour to major cities in the eastern half of the United States, concentrating on areas with large black populations. There he spoke about conditions in Jamaica and the rest of the Caribbean and met with black community leaders to hear their views on racial relations. After a year, he returned to Harlem and established a New York chapter of the UNIA. This eventually became the organization's international headquarters.

To help spread the UNIA's message, Garvey in 1918 began publishing the newspaper *Negro World*. It covered the UNIA's activities and reported issues and events that were of interest to blacks. Garvey wrote many of the articles that focused on important figures in black history. Distributed worldwide, the paper gradually saw its circulation rise to 60,000.

The energetic Garvey managed to make the UNIA grow quickly. By 1919, he claimed that the organization had a membership of 2 million in 30 chapters around the world. He urged black audiences at his Harlem headquarters, a large auditorium called Liberty Hall, and on his speaking tours to take pride in themselves and their appearance and to stop emulating whites. He told them to regard members of their race as heroes and to worship God as a black divine being.

Garvey's message of black pride was just what tens of thousands of black Americans wanted to hear. In an era when racial relations were growing worse by the day, he became a hero to them. Before long, he was bearing the nickname Black Moses.

In 1919, Garvey established the Negro Factories Corporation to encourage black-owned businesses. That same year, he announced the formation of the Black Star Line shipping company. It would be owned and operated exclusively by blacks, he said, and would mark the start of a movement to achieve black economic independence.

As soon as advertisements for the shipping line were placed in *Negro World*, money to finance the business began to pour in. Stock in the Black Star Line cost $5 a share, and within the line's first year more than $600,000 was raised. Much more money would follow.

In late 1919, Garvey took time out from his busy activities to marry his secretary, Amy Ashwood, in a lavish ceremony at Liberty Hall. After the marriage ended in divorce two years later, he married his new secretary, Amy Jacques, with whom he had two children, Marcus, Jr., and Julius.

Garvey, however, was always wedded to the UNIA. To capitalize on the organization's rise, he held a 30-day international convention of black organizations that commenced on August 1, 1920, in New York. Black delegates came from as far as Africa, and they witnessed quite a show in celebration of the opening of the convention. Garvey, dressed in a fancy uniform and a plumed hat, led a spectacular parade of hundreds of uniformed marchers through the streets of Harlem. That night, all of them packed Madison Square Garden to hear Garvey speak.

By the convention's end, Garvey was beginning to form an ambitious plan to establish a black homeland in Africa. It would become known as the Back to Africa movement.

But as Garvey's dreams grew, so did his troubles, for the Black Star Line turned into a humiliating fiasco. His critics demanded to know what had become of the large sums of money that investors had put into his shipping business. Then the U.S. government stepped forward, and in early 1922 Garvey was indicted for using the mail to deceive Black Star Line investors. One year later, a jury found him guilty of mail fraud. He was fined $1,000 and was sentenced to five years in prison. In February 1925, after an appeal to have his conviction overturned was rejected, he surrendered to federal authorities and was taken to the Atlanta Federal Penitentiary.

Garvey was not forgotten by his faithful followers, who held protest rallies and flooded government offices with letters and petitions in their effort to convince the authorities to release him. It was the opinion of many that Garvey had been imprisoned only because he had become a strong black leader who posed a threat to white America. To put an end to the furor, U.S. president Calvin Coolidge ordered Garvey released from prison in late 1927 and had him deported to Jamaica.

Back in his homeland, Garvey attempted to build up the branches of the UNIA outside the United States. He managed to found a chapter in Europe and to organize a successful UNIA convention in Kingston in 1929. But for the most part, his golden touch was gone. The American branches missed his

strong presence, and without his leadership, the organization collapsed.

For a few years, Garvey turned to local politics,
serving several terms on Kingston's governing council. In the late 1930s, he made one last push to rebuild
the UNIA. But there would be no more rallies or
parades.

On June 10, 1940—five months after he had suffered a serious stroke while in London—Marcus Garvey died at the age of 53. He was laid to rest in
England. But in 1964, in accordance with his last
wishes, his body was returned to Jamaica, where he
was given the country's highest honor, the title of first
national hero.

SOJOURNER TRUTH

Antislavery actvist Sojourner Truth was born into slavery around 1797 in Hurley, New York. Her name was originally Isabella, and she was the ninth child of the slaves Betsey and James. By the time of her birth, her older brothers and sisters had already been sold to other slaveholders.

Home for Isabella was a damp cellar on the Hardenbergh's farm near the Hudson River in upstate

New York. Her mother, being a deeply religious woman, taught Isabella that if she led an upright life, God
would always watch over her. Yet when Isabella was
11, her master separated her from her parents and her
younger brother, Peter. She was sold to John Nealy,
who owned a store and dock in nearby Kingston.

Life at her new home was hard for Isabella. She did
not know how to speak English because her previous
owners, the Hardenberghs, had spoken solely Dutch;
so she was frequently beaten for not being able to
follow her new masters' orders. Nealy and his wife
attempted to teach Isabella English. But their efforts
failed, and they grew frustrated. One Sunday morning, John Nealy beat Isabella severely with metal
rods he had heated in a fire. When her father got
wind of this brutal punishment, he persuaded Martin
Schryver, a local fisherman and tavern owner, to buy
her from the Nealys.

Isabella worked on the Schryvers' farm and helped
them bring in catches of fish. Under her new owners'
guidance, she became relatively fluent in English. She
never learned to read or write, however, and her
speech was always marked by a strong Dutch accent.

In 1810, the Schryvers sold Isabella to John
Dumont, a farmer who lived in nearby New Paltz. He
was not a harsh master, but his wife took an instant
dislike to Isabella and treated her cruelly. Isabella
remembered her mother's advice, however, to repay
evil with good, believing that her hard work would
eventually be rewarded.

In her middle teens, Isabella fell in love with a young
slave named Robert, who lived on a neighboring es-
tate. Their romance was forbidden by Robert's owner,

who beat the boy senseless for visiting her. Not long afterward, she agreed to become the wife of Thomas, one of Dumont's older slaves. Their first child, Diana, was born in 1815; and during the next 12 years, Isabella had four more children: Elizabeth, Hannah, Peter, and Sophie. When they were infants, they usually went with her into the fields, strapped to her back.

Isabella taught each of her children the lessons about hard work and faith that she had learned from her mother. As she continued to labor for the Dumonts, rumors began to spread that slavery would be outlawed in New York State. Finally, in 1824, the state legislature passed an emancipation law. Under its provisions, Isabella would become eligible to receive her freedom in 1827.

Isabella was ecstatic that her prayers had been answered, and she became even more industrious when her master told her that he would free her a year earlier if she worked especially hard. When 1826 came, however, he went back on his promise. Isabella promptly decided to escape.

One day that autumn, without telling her husband or children, Isabella gathered some food and clothes, took hold of baby Sophie, and left the Dumont farm. She found shelter at the home of a Quaker couple, the Van Wageners. And when Dumont came looking for her, the Van Wageners bought her and Sophie for a small sum, then set them free.

The grateful Isabella remained at the Van Wageners' house as a domestic servant. Meanwhile, she turned her attention to freeing her other children. She soon learned that her son, Peter, had been sold to a man named Gedney, who had sent the boy south, violating a New York law that forbade transporting slaves out of state. In the spring of 1828, with the help of antislavery activists, she successfully sued Gedney for Peter's return and became one of the first black women in the country to win a court case.

During the two years that Isabella worked for the Van Wageners, she settled her differences with the Dumonts and was allowed to visit with her three older daughters. Her husband, who had been emancipated in 1827, had chosen to go his own way.

Isabella's strong religious faith prompted her to join the local Methodist church. There she met a schoolteacher who was planning to move to New York City and offered to help Isabella find work. Isabella and Peter moved to New York City in the summer of 1828, joining the swelling number of former slaves who had come to the city in search of jobs. Isabella was hired as a servant, and Peter enrolled in a navigation trade school.

Isabella soon joined the Zion African church, which encouraged its members to talk openly about their religious feelings. She became known for her loud and vigorous testimonials and for her ability to recite biblical passages. As the years passed, she heard voices telling her that she had a mission to help the needy and the oppressed. And in June 1843, she left New York City to become a traveling preacher, bearing the new name she had given herself, Sojourner Truth.

Truth slowly made her way to New England, where she became increasingly involved in the antislavery crusade. When it was suggested to her that a published account of her life as a slave, stressing her profound faith in God, would be uplifting to many people,

Truth agreed to tell her story. In 1850, *The Narrative of Sojourner Truth*, which included an introduction by the noted abolitionist William Lloyd Garrison, was published. The book made Truth widely known, and Garrison promptly persuaded her to become a traveling lecturer for the abolitionist cause throughout New England.

Truth was also interested in another cause: equal political and legal rights for women. In the United States in the 1840s, women could not vote or hold political office, were paid far less than male workers, and had few educational opportunities. A married woman and her property were entirely under her husband's control; in the event of divorce, the husband was always given custody of the children.

Truth readily embraced the women's rights movement, led by Susan B. Anthony, Lucretia Mott, Lucy Stone, and other prominent feminists. Many of them were also active in the Underground Railroad, the network of people who helped runaway slaves escape to the North. Truth was well aware that women and slaves endured similar hardships, and her speeches at abolitionist meetings forcefully pointed out that she continued to be oppressed even after she had become a free woman.

In 1848, feminists held the first national women's rights convention, in Seneca Falls, New York. There they drew up a plan for helping women achieve equality with men. Truth did not attend the convention, but she went to many other women's rights meetings, and in 1850 she addressed that year's national women's rights conference. Two years later, at the national conference in Akron, Ohio, she gave one of her most famous speeches. Stating that the work she had done throughout her life was equal to any man's, she cited a list of accomplishments, punctuating each achievement with the refrain "And ain't I a woman?"

By the mid-1850s, Sojourner Truth's name was known throughout much of America. Her audiences were not always friendly or even courteous, and sometimes she was jeered by opponents of both of her causes. But nothing deterred her from delivering her message. In 1857, Truth moved to Battle Creek, Michigan, a town with strong abolitionist roots that had always given her a favorable reception. Two of her daughters and their families later moved to Battle Creek to be near her.

Following the outbreak of the Civil War in 1861, Truth toured the Midwest to rouse support for the Union war effort. As always, she supported herself by occasionally hiring herself out as a domestic servant. But when the 66-year-old Truth became too ill to work in 1863, friends collected enough money for her to buy a small house in Battle Creek.

The following year, with her health vastly improved, Truth journeyed to Washington, D.C., where she met with President Abraham Lincoln and personally thanked him for all he had done on the behalf of black Americans. She remained in the nation's capital to counsel freed blacks, and after the Civil War ended in 1865, she worked as an administrator at the Freedmen's Hospital, run by the Freedmen's Bureau, the federal agency established to help former slaves.

In 1868, she launched what proved to be an unsuccessful campaign to persuade Congress to grant land in the West to black settlers.

Sojourner Truth returned to Michigan in the early 1870s and spent her remaining years among family and friends. She died in Battle Creek on November 26, 1883.

HARRIET TUBMAN

Antislavery activist Harriet Tubman was born as the slave Harriet Ross around 1820 on a plantation on Maryland's Eastern Shore. Put to work as a household servant at five, she was roughly treated, ill clothed, and always hungry. At the age of seven, she stole a piece of sugar, then fled in terror from her mistress's rage. Starving and fearful, the little girl returned after hiding in a pigpen for five days. Her "lady" gave her a savage whipping.

In 1835, an overseer ordered 15-year-old Harriet to hold a slave he intended to whip. She refused, and the slave ran, prompting the enraged overseer to hurl a lead weight at him. The missile struck Harriet, severely gashed her head, and put her into a coma for weeks. For the rest of her life, she carried a deep scar and suffered from what she called "sleeping fits": without warning, she would fall unconscious for hours at a time.

In 1844, Harriet Ross married John Tubman, a free black man, but she remained a slave. Her greatest fear was being "sold south"—sent to live on an Alabama or Mississippi cotton plantation where slaves' lives were shorter and even more brutal than in Maryland. In 1849, Tubman's worst fears materialized: two of her sisters were led south in irons. She knew she would meet the same fate unless she acted quickly.

During the 1830s, antislavery activists had set up a network of houses where slaves could hide as they fled northward to freedom. Known as the Underground Railroad—its safe houses were "stations"; its guides, "conductors"—the network helped thousands of people escape.

Tubman had heard stories of the Underground Railroad; when she learned that she too had been sold south, she decided to flee. Saying nothing to John Tubman—who had not only forbidden her to escape, but threatened to report her—she packed a bit of cornbread, anxiously glanced at the moonless autumn sky, and headed north. Hiding by day, traveling by night, sometimes stopping at "stations" along the route, Tubman trudged through some 90 miles of swamp and forest. Many painful days after she started, she reached Pennsylvania and stood on free soil at last. "I felt like I was in heaven," she said later. She resolved to bring the rest of her family north as soon as she could.

Tubman made her way to Philadelphia, got a job as a dishwasher, saved her money, and kept her ears open. Learning of the Philadelphia Vigilance Committee, an organization that helped fugitive slaves, she began visiting its office. There, she talked with abolitionists, listened to fugitive slaves' stories, and plotted ways to set her family free. She found such a way in 1850, when a Maryland abolitionist asked the Vigilance Committee to help a black woman and her two children escape from Baltimore. Listening to his description, the astonished Tubman realized that the woman was her sister Mary. Although committee leaders feared for Tubman's life, she insisted on bringing the family out herself. Making the first of at least 19 daring rescue missions, she slipped into Maryland and led her passengers back safely.

On one of her perilous conducting trips to the Eastern Shore, Tubman tried to persuade John Tubman to go north with her, but he had taken a new wife and refused. Tubman never saw her husband again and rarely spoke of him, but for the rest of her life she identified herself as Mrs. Tubman.

After Congress passed the Fugitive Slave Act of 1850, bounty hunters captured more and more runaways in Philadelphia. Aware of the great danger, Tubman's friends persuaded her to move to St. Catharines, Canada, in 1851. She now faced a 500-

mile journey each time she traveled to the Eastern Shore. Her standard procedure was to gather money and supplies, then steal down the coast to Delaware and into Maryland. There she would make contact with slaves who were ready to escape. She usually started them north on a Saturday night, hoping they would not be missed and pursued until Monday. Before heading out, she paid someone to take down the Wanted posters that would be sure to appear across the countryside.

Tubman knew all the places to hide: along with the Underground Railroad's safe houses, there were drainage ditches, hedges, abandoned sheds, and tobacco barns. Merciful and humane, Tubman could also be tough: she always carried a revolver, and if a passenger grew fainthearted, she would hold the gun to his or her head and bark, "Move or die!" Tubman's work earned her the nickname Moses, after the biblical prophet who had brought his people out of bondage and into the Promised Land.

In the course of her crusade, Tubman met many abolitionist leaders, including Frederick Douglass, John Brown, and U.S. senator William Seward. A great admirer of Tubman's, Seward presented her with the deed to a small house in the upstate New York village of Auburn, in 1857. Auburn, a major Underground Railroad station, became Tubman's home for the rest of her life.

Not long after moving there, Tubman learned that her father was to be tried for helping another slave escape. Hurrying south, she "borrowed" a horse and wagon, sped to the plantation, and drove off with her amazed parents, whom she later settled in Auburn. To support them and herself, she worked full-time as a hotel chambermaid when she was not traveling. Whenever she could, she addressed antislavery meetings, where highly educated audiences listened spellbound to speeches by the illiterate former slave.

As thousands of slaves fled their masters, the South called for ever more rigorous enforcement of the Fugitive Slave Law. In 1860, Tubman made what would be her last, and perhaps most dangerous, trip on the Underground Railroad. She returned with seven men and women, then, at the insistence of friends, crossed the Canadian border.

After the Civil War broke out in 1861, Tubman traveled to Beaufort, South Carolina, to care for the thousands of slaves who had been abandoned by their masters and were now flooding Union army camps. Working in a makeshift hospital, she nursed ailing, malnourished blacks as well as wounded white soldiers. From Beaufort, Tubman went to a Florida military hospital, where she treated soldiers and former slaves suffering from dysentery, smallpox, and malaria.

In the spring of 1863, union officers assigned Tubman to a new job: spy. Shifting her base to South Carolina, she guided a small expedition deep into enemy territory and returned with invaluable intelligence on Confederate encampments. That summer, she conducted her most celebrated exploit, leading a raid up the Combahee River to destroy enemy-held railroads and bridges and to cut off Confederate supplies and troops. A phenomenal success, the exploit cost the enemy millions of dollars and 800 slaves.

During the next year, Tubman participated in numerous guerrilla operations for the Union Army. Visiting her parents while on leave in 1864, she suffered an intense bout of the sleeping seizures that had continued to plague her; but by early spring, 1865, she felt well enough to return to the South. This time, she operated out of Washington, D.C., serving as a nurse for the U.S. Sanitary Commission, an early version of the Medical Corps.

The Civil War ended in April, and that summer Tubman returned to Auburn. On the train home, she received her first shocking hint of the new battle that lay ahead for black Americans: when she presented her half-fare military pass to the white northern conductors, they not only refused to honor it, they shoved her into the baggage car, severely injuring her arm. Blacks, they said, rated no special privileges.

Although Tubman had been entitled to military pay for her services as a scout and nurse, she had neither requested nor received it. Now 45 years old, she was penniless, responsible for her aged parents, and in steady pain from her wrenched arm. Presenting Tubman's carefully saved records as evidence, Seward and other influential officials petitioned the government for the money it owed her, but the payment never came through. With the help of well-to-do neighbors, the undaunted Tubman continued to feed, clothe, and nurse the stream of impoverished blacks who appeared at her door.

In 1869, Tubman married Nelson Davis, a 25-year-old former slave and soldier she had met during the war. For many years, she supported her tubercular husband by selling vegetables from her garden. In 1890, two years after Davis's death, the government awarded her $8 per month as a Civil War veteran's widow.

In the 1890s, Tubman vigorously supported Susan B. Anthony and the women's rights movement, and in 1908, she reached a long-held goal by establishing a home for sick and needy black people. On March 10, 1913, the Underground Railroad's most famous conductor, who proudly asserted that she had "never lost a passenger," died in Auburn at the age of 93.

BOOKER T. WASHINGTON

Educator and racial spokes-
man Booker Taliaferro Washington was born a slave
on April 5, 1856, near Hales Ford, Virginia. He received his last name from the slave Washington
Ferguson, whom his mother, Jane, married in 1860.
Booker never knew who his real father was, although
the man was almost certainly white.

Home for Booker was a 200-acre farm, where he handled some of the heavier chores as soon as he was able. He lived in a squalid cabin that had empty cupboards and no stove. His bed was the dirt floor.

The slaves' world changed dramatically—in theory, at least—on April 9, 1865, when the Civil War ended, leaving all blacks free to go their own way. For many of these former slaves, however, there was nowhere to go. Poor and never given the chance to get an education, they had few prospects of finding new employment.

Booker's stepfather was luckier than most. He found work as a salt packer in Malden, West Virginia, where he was joined by Jane and her three children, Booker, John, and Amanda. It was not long before a fourth child came into the family, an orphan boy named James.

Like their stepfather, Booker and John went to work in the mine, shoveling salt into barrels. The work was backbreaking, and it left Booker with only one hope: to get an education and free himself from a life of slavelike labor. Fortunately for him, a school for blacks was established in the nearby community of Tinkersville not long after he arrived in West Virginia. He began to attend classes at night, after his workday was done.

In 1872, 16-year-old Booker T. Washington made a decision that would shape the rest of his life. Determined to make something of himself, he traveled more than 200 miles—most of them on foot—to Hampton, Virginia, the site of Hampton Normal and Agricultural Institute, a large industrial school for blacks. He arrived there with only 50 cents in his pocket and an appetite to learn. In recognition of his drive and desire, he was permitted to pay his way through school by working as a janitor.

Washington remained at Hampton Institute for three years. The school emphasized self-discipline, morality, personal hygiene, and what its founder, General Samuel Armstrong, called the "routine of industrious habits." He believed that the key to racial advancement was the acquisition of practical trade skills, which would help blacks become contributing members of society and enable them to win the respect of whites. It was a theory that Washington would also adopt. Indeed, he learned his lessons so well that in 1875, when he graduated from Hampton, he was asked to deliver the commencement address.

Washington then returned to the Tinkersville school, this time as a teacher, and put into practice what he had learned at Hampton. He left his job in 1878 to enroll at a Baptist seminary in Washington, D.C., but after half a year he was convinced that his future lay in education, not the ministry. When Armstrong invited him to join the Hampton faculty in the fall of 1879, he jumped at the chance.

Washington proved to be such an able and popular educator that Armstrong wholeheartedly recommended him for the post of principal at a new black school in Tuskegee, Alabama. He arrived in the southern town in June 1881 eager to begin work but was dismayed to find that the school had not yet been built. Washington set to work at once getting the school off the ground. To the townpeople's astonishment, he opened the Tuskegee Normal and Industrial Institute on July 4, 1881, just 10 days after his arrival.

Classes for the students were held in a large shack while Washington raised the down payment for a permanent site, an old farm outside of town. As soon as the property was purchased, he and his pupils set to work constructing their own school brick by brick.

At first, Tuskegee Institute's primary goal was to prepare its students to teach in black elementary schools. But Washington gradually broadened the curriculum to include vocational courses, much like those at Hampton. Academic subjects were reinforced with practical learning: math students measured floors for new carpets; English students wrote essays on cabinetry or dressmaking. When deposits of brick clay were discovered on the school's land, brickmaking became part of the curriculum. In time, the Tuskegee kiln became a major industry, selling the bricks that were not used in the construction of new campus buildings to people throughout the county.

Washington had help in making the institute's enrollment grow. Fanny Smith, his longtime sweetheart, married him in 1882 and devoted herself to the school. She gave birth to a daughter, Portia, in 1883 and died the following year. Sadly, Washington was beset by tragedy again a few years later. In 1885, he married Olivia Davidson, Tuskegee's first "lady principal," who bore him two sons, Booker, Jr., and Ernest Davidson. Her health failed after the birth of Ernest, and she died in 1889. Two years later, Washington married for a final time. His third wife was Margaret Murray, who had replaced Olivia as principal.

By the 1890s, Washington had built Tuskegee into the largest and best-endowed black institution in America. He promptly used his reputation for being a successful educator as a springboard to national prominence. Washington had devoted his adult life to working to uplift his race, and at the 1895 Cotton States and International Exposition in Atlanta, Georgia, he gave the speech that marked him as America's leading black spokesman.

Addressing an audience of several thousand with what has become known as the Atlanta Compromise, Washington exhorted blacks to postpone their demands for equal rights and focus on improving themselves through education, industriousness, and racial solidarity. "In all things that are purely social," he said, "we can be as separate as the fingers, yet one as the hand in all things essential to mutual progress." Requiring no change in the existing social order, his program for racial progress for blacks won the support of white society and opened the door to black opportunity. During the next two decades, U.S. presidents Grover Cleveland, William McKinley, and Theodore Roosevelt all sought his advice on black issues.

Washington found many ways to make his views felt. In 1900, he founded the National Negro Business League, which quickly evolved into a highly successful organization that promoted black business. The following year, the story of his life, the now-classic *Up from Slavery*, was published; it inspired Americans of every color and prompted some of the nation's most influential philanthropists to assist the black cause. In fact, his status as the nation's most important black leader enabled him to build the Tuskegee Machine, a powerful group of politicians, businessmen, philan-

thropists, and educators who helped advance the Tuskegee president's doctrines.

Washington certainly had his opponents, chief
among them the highly educated scholar and activist
W. E. B. Du Bois. Maintaining that Washington's
industrial program stunted the intellectual growth
of their race, Du Bois called on the educated black
elite to provide strong leadership in the fight for
racial justice and demanded that blacks be immediately granted their full civil rights. By the early 1900s,
the black community was divided between Washington's camp and Du Bois's.

For the rest of his life, Washington jockeyed with
his rivals for control of black America. He continued
to stress the importance of accommodation, education, and economic advancement within the black
community. But his message fell increasingly on deaf
ears. His program was not working; accommodationist polices were not leading to black advancement.

In his last few years, Washington kept up his gruel-
ing pace as an educator and leader of his race. But he
also began to speak out against racism more forcefully
than ever before. Unfortunately, his attempts to expose the ugliness of racism did not have much impact.
An accommodationist at heart, he could never attack
the system of white supremacy with any real vigor.

By 1915, Washington's health had been failing
for some time. In early November, he collapsed in
New York City during a fundraising tour. He insisted
on returning home to Tuskegee, where he died on
November 13, at the age of 59. It was an apt resting

place for this latter-day Moses, who achieved the highest position of influence ever held by a black American.

Richard Allen

Frazier, Edward Franklin. *The Negro Church in America*. New York: Schocken Books, 1974.

Klots, Steve. *Richard Allen*. New York: Chelsea House, 1991.

Mary McLeod Bethune

Franklin, John H., and August Meier, eds. *Black Leaders of the Twentieth Century*. Urbana: University of Illinois Press, 1982.

Halasa, Malu. *Mary Mcleod Bethune*. New York: Chelsea House, 1989.

Meltzer, Milton. *Mary McLeod Bethune: Voice of Black Hope*. New York: Viking, 1987.

Frederick Douglass

Quarles, Benjamin. *Frederick Douglass*. New York: Atheneum, 1976.

Russell, Sharman. *Frederick Douglass*. New York: Chelsea House, 1988.

Sundquist, Eric J., ed. *Frederick Douglass: New Literary and Historical Essays*. New York: Cambridge University Press, 1990.

W. E. B. Du Bois

Aptheker, Herbert, ed. *Annotated Bibliography of the Published Writings of W. E. B. Du Bois*. Millwood, NY: Kraus-Thomson, 1973.

Du Bois, W. E. B. *The Souls of Black Folk: Essays and Sketches*. 1903. Reprint. New York: Vintage Books/Library of America, 1990.

Stafford, Mark. *W. E. B. Du Bois*. New York: Chelsea House, 1989.

Marcus Garvey

Garvey, Amy Jacques, ed. *Philosophy and Opinions of Marcus Garvey*. New York: Atheneum, 1986.

Lawler, Mary. *Marcus Garvey*. New York: Chelsea House, 1988.

Nembhard, Len S. *Trials and Triumphs of Marcus Garvey*. New York: Kraus Reprint Co., 1978.

Sojourner Truth

Corbin, Carole L. *The Right To Vote*. New York: Franklin Watts, 1985.

Dunster, Mark. *Sojourner Truth*. Fresno, CA: Linden Publications, 1983.

Krass, Peter. *Sojourner Truth*. New York: Chelsea House, 1988.

Harriet Tubman

Blockson, Charles L. *The Underground Railroad*. New York: Prentice Hall, 1987.

McPherson, James M. *Battle Cry of Freedom*. New York: Oxford University Press, 1988.

Taylor, M. W. *Harriet Tubman*. New York: Chelsea House, 1991.

Booker T. Washington

Harlan, Louis R. *Booker T. Washington: The Wizard of Tuskegee, 1901–1915*. New York: Oxford University Press, 1983.

Schroeder, Alan. *Booker T. Washington*. New York, Chelsea House, 1992.

Washington, Booker T. *Up from Slavery*. 1901. Reprint. New York: Viking Penguin, 1986.

❧ INDEX ❧

RICHARD RENNERT has edited the nearly 100 volumes in Chelsea House's award-winning BLACK AMERICANS OF ACHIEVEMENT series, which tells the stories of black men and women who have helped shape the course of modern history. He is also the author of several sports biographies, including *Henry Aaron*, *Jesse Owens*, and *Jackie Robinson*. He is a graduate of Haverford College in Haverford, Pennsylvania.